GCSE PERFORMANCE PIECES
DRUMS

SERIES EDITOR: ANDREW S. COXON
COMPILED BY: NOAM LEDERMAN

PLAYBACK+
Speed • Pitch • Balance • Loop

To acces audio visit:
www.halleonard.com/mylibrary
Enter Code:
1861-4751-2732-2656

ISBN 978-1-78038-642-3

R● RHINEGOLD EDUCATION

EXCLUSIVELY DISTRIBUTED BY
HAL•LEONARD®

For all works contained herein:
Unauthorized copying, arranging, adapting, recording, internet posting, public performance,
or other distribution of the music in this publication is an infringement of copyright.
Infringers are liable under the law.

Visit Hal Leonard Online at
www.halleonard.com

World headquarters, contact:
Hal Leonard
7777 West Bluemound Road
Milwaukee, WI 53213
Email: info@halleonard.com

In Europe, contact:
Hal Leonard Europe Limited
1 Red Place
London, W1K 6PL
Email: info@halleonardeurope.com

In Australia, contact:
Hal Leonard Australia Pty. Ltd.
4 Lentara Court
Cheltenham, Victoria, 3192 Australia
Email: info@halleonard.com.au

About the series editor **4**

About the author **4**

Introduction **5**

Drum kit notation key **7**

TAKE ME OUT *8*

DON'T LOOK BACK IN ANGER *12*

LIVIN' ON A PRAYER *17*

NO ONE KNOWS *22*

SOUL MAN *28*

COME TOGETHER *32*

JOKER & THE THIEF *37*

THE PRETENDER *43*

MASTER OF PUPPETS *49*

SOMEBODY TOLD ME *55*

ABOUT THE SERIES EDITOR

Andrew Coxon graduated from York University with a joint Honours Degree in Music and English before going on to Leeds University to complete a PGCE, and later gained a further degree through the Open University. He has had a teaching career spanning more than 40 years, for the most part as a Head of Department, and has been an examiner and moderator for many years, currently holding a senior GCSE examining position. He has recently authored music education materials for Rhinegold Education and Nelson Thornes.

Having spent most of his professional life in the North East, he now teaches part-time in Cumbria where he lives with his wife, son and a border collie. He still gains tremendous enjoyment from his classroom work, organising two instrumental groups and taking part in regular concerts, all in addition to his regular church organ-playing duties.

ABOUT THE AUTHOR

Noam Lederman has been a member of the international examination board Rockschool since 2003 and took on the role of chief examiner in January 2009. He wrote the 2006-2012 drum syllabus and was executive producer of the 2012-2018 guitar, bass and drums syllabus. In addition, Noam has produced many educational products for drums. These include playalong books for bands such as Nirvana, Deep Purple, The Who, Rush and Led Zeppelin, well-known publications such as the *Beat-O-Pedia* and *Drumming Styles* and digital apps such as *Killer Beats* and *Freestyle*.

As a professional session drummer, Noam has worked with many well-known artists and producers such as Corinne Bailey Rae, State Of Bengal, Mark Hill, Trevor Horn and others. He has performed at prominent UK and international festivals such as Womad, Glastonbury and Sonar as well as appearing on MTV.

INTRODUCTION

This book offers ten pieces for you to play. They are at a range of standards, from the equivalent of Grade 3 through to Grade 6. **However, as these pieces have not been set by any examination board thus far, grades are given as guides and you should ask your teacher to check with the GCSE examination board and/or its specification for a final ruling.**

The book contains songs in a variety of styles which cover the period from 1969 with The Beatles' 'Come Together' through to 2007 with 'The Pretender' by Foo Fighters. While many may be well-known (The Beatles or The Killers), there may well be some which are less familiar to you but, if you are willing to spend time practising them, I am sure you will really enjoy them and gain great satisfaction from being able to play them well.

'Don't Look Back in Anger' by Oasis is a good song to choose if you want to demonstrate reliable hand coordination and semiquaver fills around the drum kit, while Franz Ferdinand's 'Take Me Out' will enable you to show fast hand technique and solid open hi-hat control. Several of these songs will really allow you to 'get inside' them and be able to add fills which show a thorough understanding of the song's style.

The important thing to do when choosing what to prepare for an examination is to choose something which is comfortably within your technical abilities. It is not a good idea to choose a piece on the basis that it is hard and will, therefore, gain you a higher mark for difficulty. This may be the case but, with any examination board at GCSE, it is your ability to perform the rhythms correctly, to show mastery of the kit, to show that you understand the style and character of the piece and to demonstrate that you can perform with total confidence and conviction that will gain you most marks. You are, after all, giving a musical performance and you would not want to go to a concert to hear very difficult songs played badly!

With each piece, there is expert advice on how to approach it, what you should look out for (for example, particular techniques you will need to master) and how to shape the piece into a really musical performance. Please read this through carefully before you start on any of the pieces and be prepared to refer back to it if you need to.

I am sure you will find plenty of music in this book to enjoy and will have great success playing the wide range of songs.

Good luck!

Andrew Coxon
Series Editor

SUGGESTED LISTENING

A YouTube playlist has been created containing all the songs in this book for you to listen to. The playlist also contains any additional suggested listening the author recommends, including cover versions and wider listening to help you get a feel for each song and its cultural context. Listening to a wide range of music will help you create your own interpretation.

Access the playlist by searching YouTube for 'Rhinegold Education', where you'll find our channel and the playlist within it. Alternatively, scan this QR code with your smartphone to go straight there.

BACKING TRACKS

To access online backing tracks for every song, simply go to www.halleonard.com/mylibrary and enter the code found on page 1 of this book. This includes PLAYBACK+, a multifunctional audio player that allows you to slow down audio without changing pitch, set loop points, change keys, and pan left or right. The track order is listed on page 64.

DRUM KIT NOTATION KEY

The following system of drum kit notation is employed in this book:

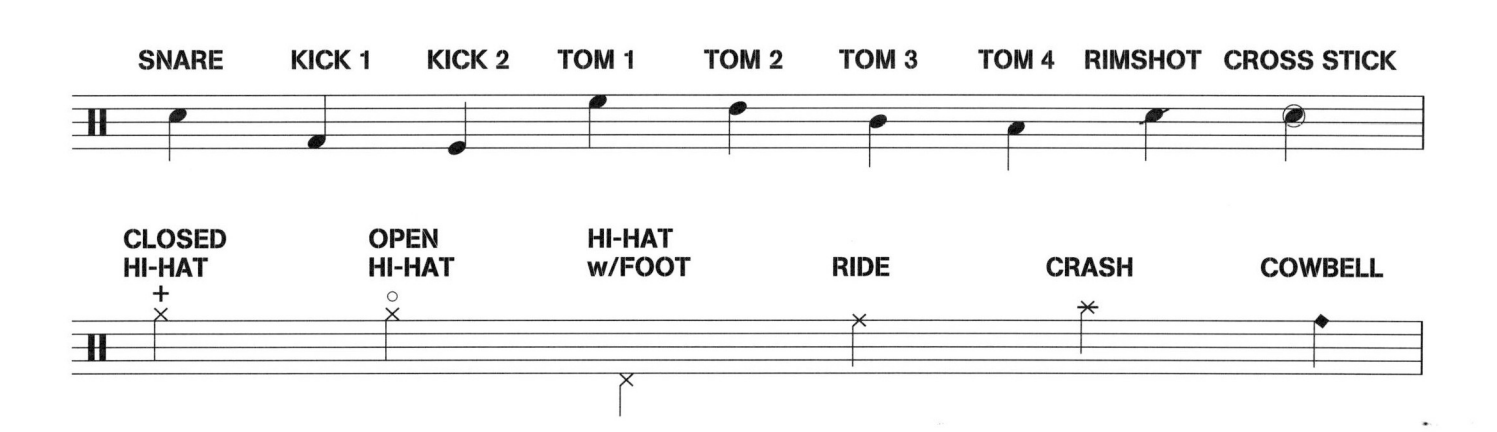

TAKE ME OUT
FRANZ FERDINAND
GRADE 3 STANDARD

'Take Me Out' is a song by the Scottish band Franz Ferdinand. It was released in 2004 as part of their self-titled debut album. The single reached Number 3 in the UK Singles chart, Number 3 in the US Modern Rock Tracks and was certified Gold by the Recording Industry Association of America. The band, formed in 2002, has released three studio albums and sold over three million albums worldwide. Franz Ferdinand is one of the few Scottish bands in history that has been nominated for Grammy Awards, Brit Awards and won an NME award.

Franz Ferdinand

This is a good song to choose if you want to demonstrate fast hand technique and solid open hi-hat control. There are two main grooves in this piece: the open hi-hat groove that starts in bar 5 and the semiquaver groove that starts in bar 23.

SONG STATS
Style: Indie Rock
Tempo: ♩=105

The open hi-hat groove requires secure coordination and balanced posture. Make sure you are sitting comfortably and start by playing only the hi-hat pattern, focusing on the timing of opening and closing the hi-hat. Aim to keep the pulse consistent and produce the two sounds clearly: closed hi-hat and open hi-hat. Ensure your posture remains balanced; leaning back or sideways when performing the open hi-hat should always be avoided as it will affect your timing and lead to bad habits in the future. When you feel that you have mastered this pattern, add the bass drum and snare, and, finally, play with the track or a metronome.

SUGGESTED LISTENING

Listening to the original recording, you'll notice this includes a slower first section which we have omitted in this arrangement so you can get straight to the fun bits.

The semiquaver groove from bar 23, with both hands on the hi-hat, is very common in this style of music. Play the semiquavers using alternate sticking R L R L (or L R L R if you are left-handed). On beats two and four, move your right hand from the hi-hat to the snare in order to play the backbeat. The key is to move the right hand quickly between positions without disturbing the pulse. When you feel comfortable with this groove, you can focus on the stylistic semiquaver note snare fills in this section. When you reach the D.S. al Coda in bar 34, go back to Segno in bar 9 and play until you see 'To Coda' where you will have to jump directly to the Coda section which starts in bar 35.

TAKE ME OUT

Words & Music by Alexander Kapranos & Nicholas McCarthy
© Copyright 2004 Universal Music Publishing Limited.
All Rights Reserved. International Copyright Secured.

2 bar count in:
♩ = 105

(Lyrics)

I say, don't you know? You say you don't know.
I say you don't know, you say you don't go.
I say you don't know, you say you don't go.

I say, take me out. I stay you don't show,
I say, take me out. If I move this could die.
I say, take me out. If I wait this could die.

don't move time is slow. I say take me out.
If eyes move this could die. I want you to take me out.
If I wane this could die. I want you to take me out.

To Coda ⊕

9

1.
E5
A5
Bm
2.
E5
Am
C6
D6
Am
I know I won't be leav - ing here.
Oh, I know I won't be
C6
D6
Am
C6
D6
leav - ing here.
I know I won't be leav - ing here.
Am
C
D7
E5
I know I won't be leav - ing here with you.
A5
Bm
D.S. al Coda
Coda
E5
A5
If I move this could die
If eyes move this could die
come on.

38
Bm7 N.C.
E5
A5
Take me out.
42
Bm
E5
45
Am
C6
D6
Am
I know I won't be leav - ing here._ Oh, I know I won't be
48
C6
D6
Am
C6
D6
leav - ing here._ I know I won't be leav - ing here._
51
Am
C
D7
Em
I know I won't be leav - ing here_ with you.
54
E5

DON'T LOOK BACK IN ANGER
OASIS
GRADE 3 STANDARD

Oasis

The English rock band Oasis was formed in Manchester in 1991. The band has had eight Number 1 singles, eight UK Number 1 albums and won fifteen NME Awards, nine Q Awards, four MTV Europe Music Awards and six Brit Awards. As of 2009, the band has sold 70 million records worldwide. 'Don't Look Back In Anger' was one of the Number 1 singles from the album *(What's the Story) Morning Glory?*, which was the second studio album by the band. The song was the first Oasis single to feature Noel Gallagher on lead vocals as well as guitar.

SONG STATS
Style: Rock
Tempo: ♩=84

This is a good song to choose if you want to demonstrate reliable hand coordination and semiquaver fills around the drum kit. Try working on the basic groove at a slower tempo until all quavers are accurate and the pattern is fluent. Then, increase the tempo gradually and focus on the balance between the hi-hat, snare and bass drum. Pay attention to the tom sections in bars 13-18 and 44-49 and the semiquaver fills in this piece. Ensure that the sticking patterns you choose to perform the fills are logical and suit your technique.

SUGGESTED LISTENING

Listen on YouTube to Oasis playing 'Don't Look Back In Anger' at one of their stadium tours to get a sense of the grandeur and popularity of the song.

The other main challenge of this piece is changing the lead drum voice within the groove from hi-hat to ride cymbal and even to crash cymbal from bar 56. It is important to aim for fluency and consistency of pulse when performing these changes as well as paying attention to the sound produced from each drum voice and the kit overall. When playing a crash cymbal hit on the first beat (bar 5, bar 9 and so on), it is important to maintain a steady pulse and synchronisation with the backing track. Commonly, the accented crash can lead to a pushed groove so practise slowly and ensure that your Oasis groove is solid.

DON'T LOOK BACK IN ANGER

Words & Music by Noel Gallagher
© Copyright 1995 Creation Songs Limited/Oasis Music (GB).
Sony/ATV Music Publishing.

14

36
C G Am E
2. Take me to the place where you go, where no - bo - dy knows
mf
38
F G* C Am G C G
if it's night or day. But please don't put your life in the hands
41
Am E Fmaj7 G6 C Am G
of a rock 'n' roll band who'll throw it all a - way.
44
F Fm C F Fm
I'm gon-na start a re-vo-lu - tion from my bed, 'cause you said the brains I had went to my
47
C F Fm C
head. Step out - side, 'cause sum - mer - time's in bloom.

50
Gsus4 G A♭dim Am G
Stand up be-side the fire - place,_ take that look from off_your face,_ ('cause) you ain't ev - er gon - na burn_ my_
f
53
F G
_ heart_ out._ And
Chorus
56
C G Am E
so Sal - ly can wait,_ she knows it's too late_
f
58
F G* C Am G C G
_ as she's walk - ing on by._ My soul slides a - way,_
61
Am E F G
_ but don't_ look back_ in an - ger, I heard you say._

LIVIN' ON A PRAYER
BON JOVI
GRADE 3 STANDARD

Bon Jovi

The America rock band Bon Jovi consists of the lead singer Jon Bon Jovi, guitarist Richie Sambora, keyboardist David Bryan, drummer Tico Torres and bassist Alec John Such (later replaced by Hugh McDonald). Throughout their career, the band have released eleven studio albums and sold 130 million records worldwide. They have performed more than 2,700 concerts in over 50 countries for more than 35 millions fans. 'Livin' On A Prayer' was the band's second single from the album *Slippery When Wet*, released in 1986. The song was well received on both rock and pop radio and its promotional video was extremely popular. This song has become the band's signature song and reached Number 1 in the UK, Canada, New Zealand, Norway and the US.

This is a good song to choose if you want to demonstrate your ability to play a simple groove with conviction while performing challenging fills and variations. From bar 19, there are semiquaver hi-hats within the groove: these can be played with either the left or right hand. Most rock drummers will choose to play the semiquavers with the left hand as playing them with the right hand requires a highly reliable technique. Choose the option which suits your technique best and focus on fluency and consistency. Bar 41 is another challenging moment where crotchet triplets are used. In order to play this accurately, divide the first two crotchets into three equal rhythms and hit both the floor and medium toms with conviction. Listening to the bass and guitar on the backing track will help you understand the rhythm aurally.

At the end of bar 51 there is a repeat sign. This means that after playing the first time bar (bars 49–51) you go back to bar 18 and play until you reach bar 49 again. Then, you skip the first time bar, jump directly to the second time bar (bar 52) and play until the end.

SUGGESTED LISTENING

Watch the promotional music video for this song to get a sense of the exaggerated performance typical of rock in the 1980s.

SONG STATS
Style: 80s Rock
Tempo: ♩=122

LIVIN' ON A PRAYER

Words & Music by Jon Bon Jovi, Richie Sambora & Desmond Child
© Copyright 1986 Bon Jovi Publishing/PolyGram International Music Publishing Incorporated/
Aggressive Music/Sony/ATV Tunes LLC.
Universal Music Publishing Limited/Sony/ATV Music Publishing.
All Rights Reserved. International Copyright Secured.

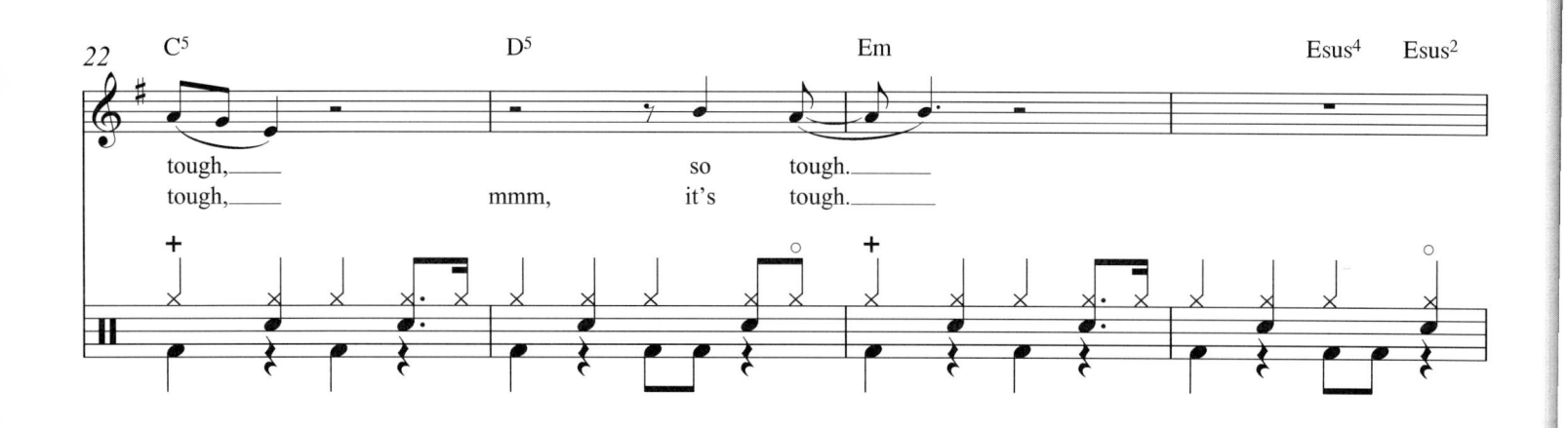

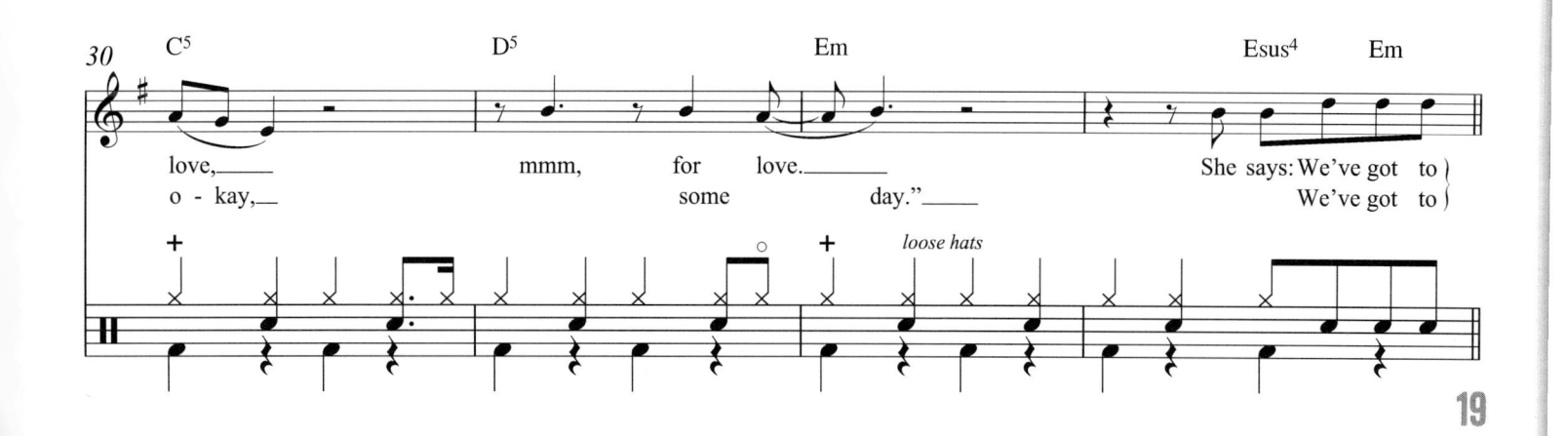

Verse

1. Tom-my used to work on the docks. Un-ion's been on strike, he's down on his luck, it's
2. Tom-my's got his six string in hock. Now he's hold-ing in when he used to make it talk so

tough, so tough.
tough, mmm, it's tough.

Gi-na works the din-er all day. Work-ing for her man, she brings home her pay for
Gi-na dreams of run-ning a-way. When she cries in the night, Tom-my whis-pers; "Ba-by it's

love, mmm, for love. She says: We've got to
o-kay, some day." We've got to

loose hats

Pre chorus
34
C5 D5 E5 C5 D5 E5
hold on to what we've got. It does - n't make a diff - 'rence if we make it or not. We've
loose hats
f
38
C5 D5 E5 C5 D5
got each oth - er, and that's a lot for love. We'll give it a shot.
3
Chorus
42
E5* C5 D5 G5 C5 D5
Whoa, we're half - way there. Oh, liv - in' on a prayer.
46
E5 C5 D5 G5 C5
Take my hand, we'll make it, I swear. Oh, liv -

1.
D5
- in' on a prayer.
2.
D5
C5
- in' on a prayer.
Liv - in' on a prayer.
Guitar solo
E5
C5
bell
D5
G5
C5
D5
E5
C5
D5
G5
C5
E5
mp cresc.

NO ONE KNOWS
QUEENS OF THE STONE AGE
GRADE 4 STANDARD

Queens of the Stone Age

The American rock band Queens of the Stone Age was formed in 1997 after the dissolution of the lead singer's previous band, Kyuss. The band plays riff-oriented heavy rock music and their sound has continually evolved to incorporate a variety of different styles and influences. QOTSA (as they are often abbreviated) have released five studio albums and were nominated four times for Best Hard Rock Performance in the Grammy awards. The song 'No One Knows' was the first single on the album *Songs for the Deaf* and the band's only single to make it to the top of the US Modern Rock charts. The iconic drumming in this song was contributed by Dave Grohl, who is most commonly known as the frontman of Foo Fighters, and prior to that as the drummer of Nirvana.

SONG STATS
Style: Heavy Rock
Tempo: ♩=170 Swung

This is a good song to choose if you want to improve your rock swing feel and triplet fills around the kit. The basic pattern is relatively simple but includes open and loose hi-hat. Loose hi-hat is also known as half open hi-hat and it is important to differentiate between this sound and the full open hi-hat sound.

The triplet fills on the snare are straightforward: focus on maintaining a consistent pulse, playing all triplet strokes evenly and planning the sticking that you want to use.

The tom fill section that starts in bar 39 is the most challenging section of the song: each two bar tom fill (bars 39-40, 43-44 and so on) will require practice and attention. Use the crotchet bass drum as the anchor and slowly work out your hand movement until you find the most logical sticking option for you. Then, using the chosen sticking pattern, work on increasing the tempo and maintaining fluency.

At the top of the drum chart you will see the rhythmic indication that all quavers should be swung. This is especially important during the groove variations and gives this simple groove a stylistic slant.

SUGGESTED LISTENING

Listen to the original track with Dave Grohl's drumming to help you achieve the right sound and feel for this song.

To play the **swing** rhythm apply a triplet feel to the quavers instead of playing them straight. This is created by playing the first and third triplets on each beat while missing the second part of the triplet.

NO ONE KNOWS

Words & Music by Josh Homme, Nick Oliveri & Mark Lanegan
© Copyright 2002 Board Stiff Music/Natural Light Music, USA/Ripplestick Music, USA.
Universal Music Publishing Limited/EMI Music Publishing Limited.
All Rights Reserved. International Copyright Secured.

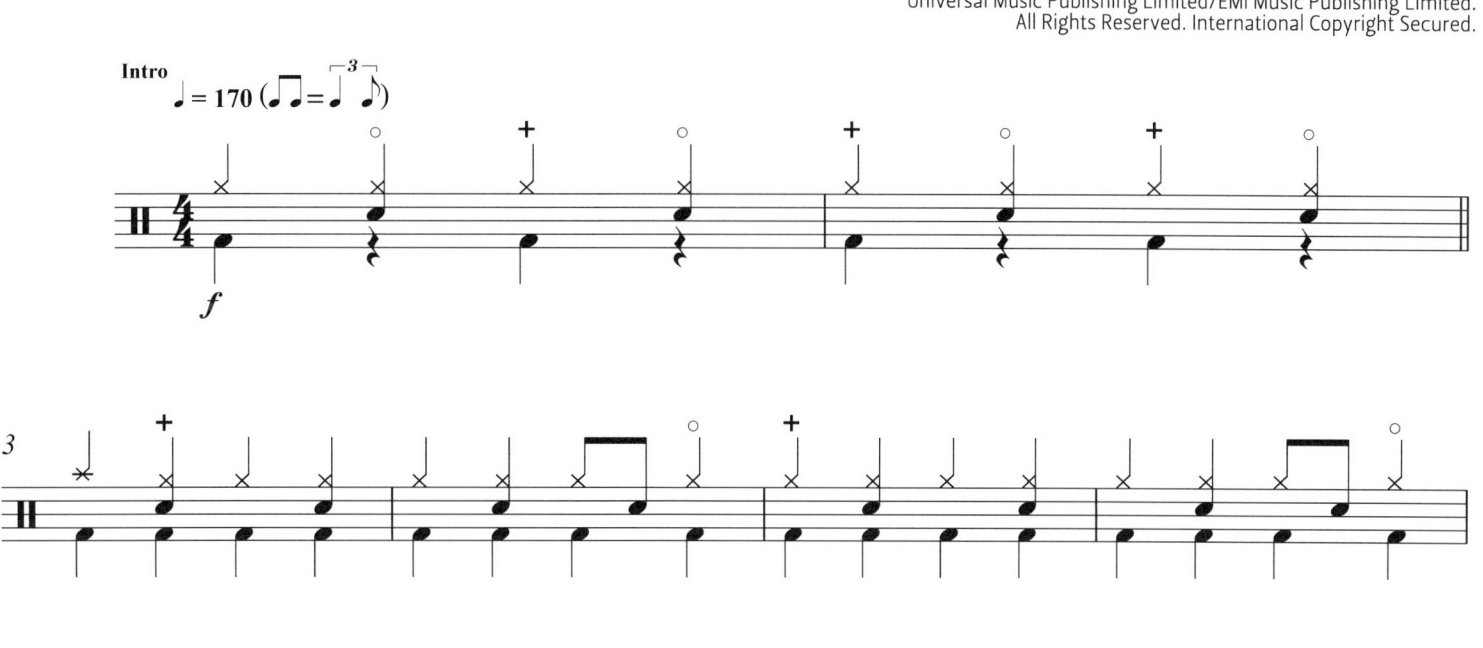

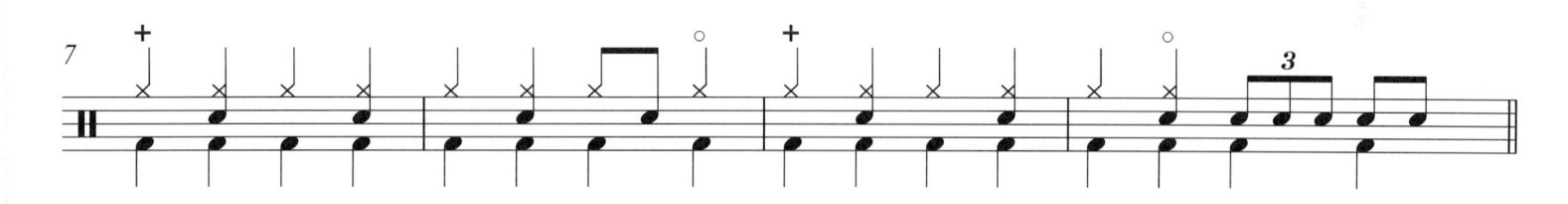

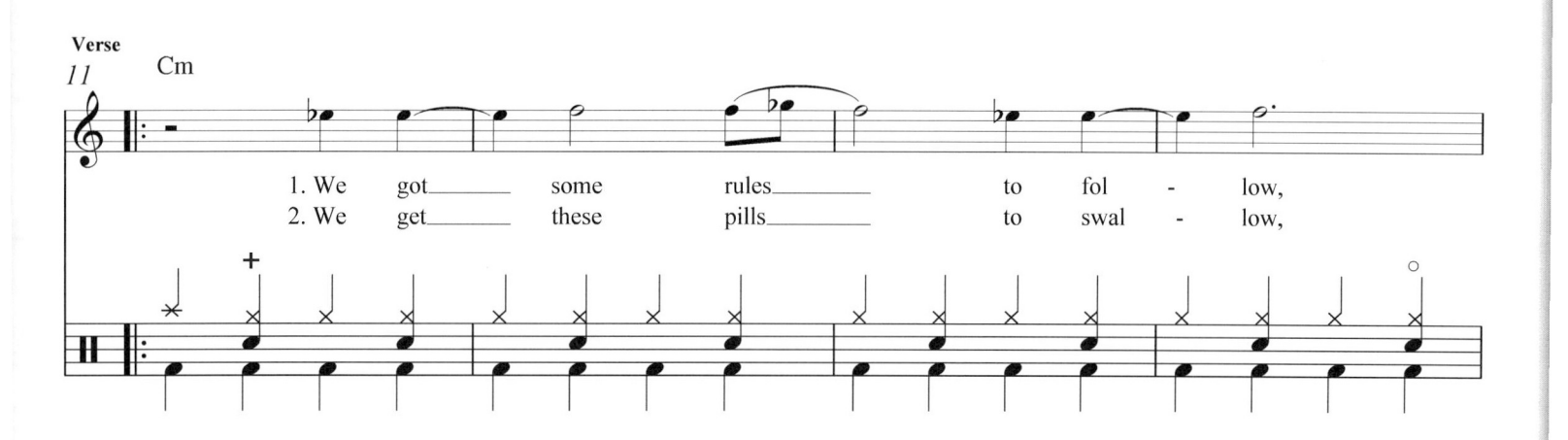

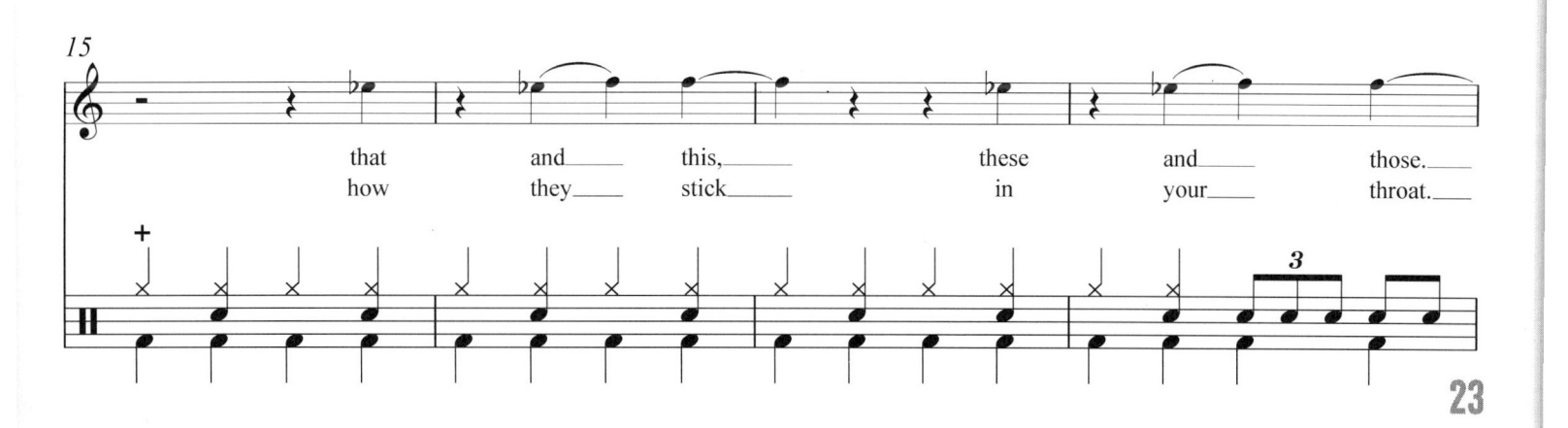

1. We got some rules to follow,
2. We get these pills to swallow,

that and this, these and those.
how they stick in your throat.

19
G7
B
No - one knows.
Taste like gold.
looser hat
1.
23
Cm
tight hat
3
2.
27
Cm
Oh, what you do
tight hat
3
31
G7
B
to me,
no - one knows.
looser hat
35
Cm
I
tight hat

Bridge
39 N.C.
G5
re - a - lise you're mine. In -
43 N.C.
G5
- deed a fool of mine. I
47 N.C.
G5
To Coda
re - a - lise you're mine. In -
51 N.C.
G5
- deed a fool of mine. Ah.

26

2.
75
Cm
Plea - sant - ly cav -
tight hat
79
G7
B
- ing in.
I come un - done.
looser hat
83
Cm
D.S. al Coda
And I
tight hat
Coda
87
N.C.
- deed a fool of
89
G5
Cm
mine.
Ah.

SOUL MAN
SAM & DAVE
GRADE 4 STANDARD

'Soul Man' was recorded in 1967 by the American soul and rhythm & blues duo Sam & Dave. The Rock & Roll Hall of Fame rates Sam & Dave as the most successful soul duo in history, with numerous chart-topping songs to their credit. These include 'Soul Man', 'Hold On, I'm Coming', 'Wrap it Up', 'I Thank You' and many others. 'Soul Man' led Sam & Dave to achieve their first Gold record and the Grammy award for Best Rhythm & Blues Group Performance. The backing band for this song was the famous instrumental R&B band Booker T. & the M.G.'s. They were the house band of Stax records and played on hundreds of recordings by artists such as Wilson Pickett, Bill Withers, Otis Redding and many more.

Sam & Dave

SONG STATS
Style: Soul, Rhythm & Blues
Tempo: ♩ = 116

This is a good song to choose if you want to demonstrate stylistic understanding and development. The main challenge in the groove is the use of semiquavers in the bass drums. However, the groove variations and use of rim shot and bell of ride should be observed too. You will be able to produce the most convincing bell of ride sound by stroking the bell with the neck/shoulder part of the drumstick. It is possible to stroke the bell from the right or left side: experiment and choose the option that feels more comfortable.

The bass drum pattern becomes busier from bar 17 and it is important to coordinate the quaver bass drums accurately with the hi-hats and backbeat snare. In addition, pay attention to the dynamic changes and ensure that the overall sound produced from the kit is balanced. Hitting the rim shot snare in the last section with conviction is essential to the development of the song. Focusing on the rim shot sound might affect the timing and balance initially but, with practice, this should become a natural technique that can be pulled out of your 'drummer's toolbox' at anytime. When repeating the section from bar 9, the part must be developed in a stylistic way. This means that variations and additions can be made but the groove should be maintained.

SUGGESTED LISTENING

Listening to various Stax songs from the same era will give you creative development ideas that will be stylistically suitable here.

SOUL MAN

Words & Music by Isaac Hayes & David Porter
© Copyright 1967 Almo Music Corporation, USA/Walden Music Incorporated, USA.
Warner/Chappell Music Limited/Universal Music Publishing Limited.
All Rights Reserved. International Copyright Secured.

13
G/D C6 G/B G/D C6 G/B
when you get it, ha, you got some - thing, so
hon - ey, don't you fret 'cause
ed - u - ca - ted at Wood - stock, when
15
G/D C6 G/B G/D C6 G/B
don't wor- - ry, 'cause I'm com - ing.
you ain't seen no - thing yet.
I start lov - ing, oh, I can't stop.
I'm a
Chorus
17
G F G
soul man, I'm a soul man.
HH loose
mf
20
F
I'm a soul man, I'm a
1-3.
4.
23
C D C D
soul man.
2. Got
3. I was

Bridge
26
E♭/B♭
B♭/D
C
Grab the rope and I'll pull you in.
Give you hope and
f
29
C/D
D♭/E♭
be your on - ly boy - friend yeah, yeah, yeah, yeah.
31
A♭
G♭
C♭
D♭
E♭
I'm talk- in' a - bout a
bell of ride
mp
Outro
35
A♭/C A♭/E♭ D♭6 A♭/C A♭/C A♭/E♭ D♭6 A♭/C A♭/C A♭/E♭ D♭6 A♭/C
(soul man,) I'm a (soul man,) and you a (soul man,) ah!
(2°) ad lib. vocal
f
1.
2.
38
A♭/C A♭/E♭
A♭/C A♭/E♭ D♭6 A♭/C A♭
(Soul man,)
A soul man!

COME TOGETHER
THE BEATLES
GRADE 4 STANDARD

The Beatles

The Beatles are the best-selling band in history with estimated sales of over one billion units. Apart from having more Number 1 albums on the British charts than any other act, they have received every major international music award and have been collectively voted as some of the most influential people of the 20th century. 'Come Together' is the opening song on the album *Abbey Road*. It reached the top of the charts in the US, peaked at Number 4 in the UK and became a rock classic worldwide.

The drumming in this song is adventurous and unorthodox. Choosing this song will give you an insight into the drumming philosophy of Ringo Starr. The opening pattern is the most challenging groove in the song. The combination of drum voices – ride cymbal, hi-hat, toms and bass drum with complex rhythms – will require planning and preparation. Use a metronome at a slower tempo to help you maintain a consistent pulse and practise the rhythms on the snare only. When these are understood, incorporate the other drum voices and focus on the sticking.

It is important to notice the dynamic changes from ***mp*** (moderately quiet) to ***mf*** (moderately loud) as well as the ***f*** (loud) and use of rim shot from bar 32. In bar 38, there are snare hits with and without rim shots, so it is a perfect opportunity to demonstrate your ability of performing these with fluency.

Another technical area to consider is the bass drum pattern in bars 11-12: playing the written rhythmic pattern accurately will require a solid bass drum technique. Whether you are using the heel down or heel up technique, the goal is similar and there is more than one way of getting there. Most rock drummers use the heel up technique and create two consecutive bass drum strokes by using the natural rebound of the beater off the drum head.

SONG STATS
Style: Sixties Rock
Tempo: ♩ = 84

SUGGESTED LISTENING

If you want to explore these techniques further, check out some of the educational resources by drummers Steve Smith and Jojo Mayer.

The **rim shot** sound, which is integral in any style of drumming, is created by hitting the snare drum head and surrounding rim at the same time. Practise this technique until you feel comfortable with it and only then add the bass drum and cymbals.

COME TOGETHER

Words & Music by John Lennon & Paul McCartney
© Copyright 1969 Sony/ATV Music Publishing.
All Rights Reserved. International Copyright Secured.

34

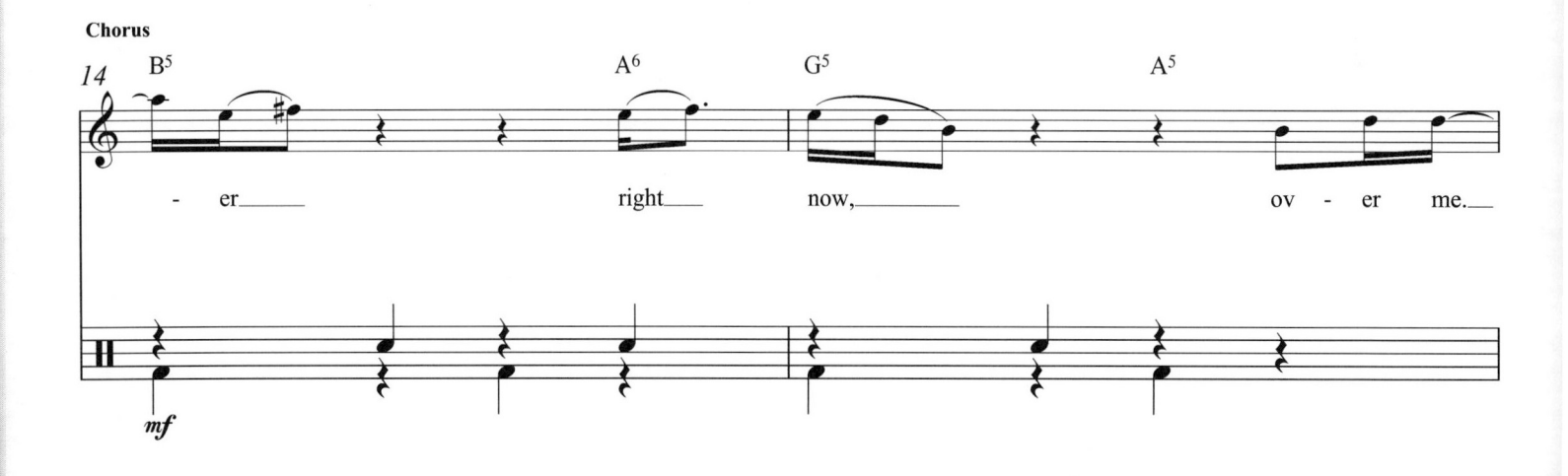

Verse
20
D5 D6 D5 D6 D5 D6 D5 D6 D5 D6 D5 D6
(3.) He bag pro - duc - tion, he got wal - rus gum - boot, he got O - no side - board, he one
(4.) not played in this arrangement.
mf
23
D5 D6 D5 D6 A5 A6 A5 A6
spi - nal crack - er. He got feet down be - low
25
A5 A6 A5 G5
his knee. Hold you in his arm - chair, you can feel his dis - ease. Come to - geth -
Chorus
28
B5 A6 G5 A5
- er right now, ov - er me.

30
Dm7
Shoot me.
mp
Interlude
32
D5 D6 D5 D6 D5 D6 D5 D6 D5 D6 D5 D6
f
35
D5 D6 D5 D6 A5 A6 A5 A6 A5 A6 A5 A6
Here it comes. Uh! Come,
38
A5 A6 A5 A6 A5 A6 A5 Dm7
come, come.

JOKER & THE THIEF
WOLFMOTHER

GRADE 5 STANDARD

Wolfmother

The Australian rock band Wolfmother released their self-titled debut album in 2006. 'Joker & the Thief', the sixth single of this album, has featured in many movies, video games, car commercials and the National Hockey League in the USA. In 2007, Wolfmother won a Grammy for Best Hard Rock Performance for the song 'Woman'.

The first part of the introduction includes triplet patterns on the hi-hat. There are various sticking options that you can use. The two most common approaches are:

1) *Alternating hands* – starting with your leading hand (R for a right hand drummer, L for a left hand drummer) and continue to alternate throughout the pattern.
2) *Maintaining the leading hand on the beat*. If you want to follow this approach use the following sticking: R L R R L. However, it is important that you experiment and choose the option that suits your technique best.

The main groove has swung quaver notes on the snare drum. These notes are marked with brackets to indicate that they are ghost notes. Ghost notes should be played at a lower dynamic level than the other strokes. The most straightforward way of achieving this sound is by keeping the drumstick close to the drum head. This type of stroke is refered to as a 'tap'. Coordinating the ghost notes with the rest of the groove is a skill, and, when done well, it significantly contributes to the fluency and movement of the groove.

The chorus groove that starts in bar 57 consists of a broken triplet pattern on the hi-hat. The rhythm of this hi-hat pattern is exactly the same as the crotchet triplets that you played on the toms in the introduction. Focus on coordinating this pattern accurately with the bass drum and snare, and practise with the backing track.

The 'choke' technique that appears in bar 25 is very common in this style of music. The most straightforward way of doing it will be to hit the cymbal with one hand while preparing to catch it with the other. However, there are many other factors to consider such as your set up, position of the cymbal you want to 'choke' and your individual technical abilities.

Choke: After hitting the crash cymbal you need to catch it and stop it from ringing (choke).

Ghost notes are played by striking the drum or cymbal very lightly. Most commonly, ghost notes are played on the snare drum with clear dynamic level distinction between them and the other snare strokes. Ghost notes can be created naturally by keeping the drumstick close to the drum head. This type of stroke is referred to as a 'tap' in the drumming world.

Flam: The flam rudiment is created by two single strokes that are played almost simultaneously. The first stroke is a quieter grace note followed by a louder primary stroke, this rudiment is played with alternative sticking (LR or RL). From bar 12 there are crotchet triplet flams on the toms. Focus on the rhythms and aim to achieve a consistent flam sound from the toms.

SUGGESTED LISTENING

If you want to improve your hard rock swung feel and perform some epic flams on the toms, this is the song for you. Listen to the original to hear how the techniques are carried out.

JOKER & THE THIEF

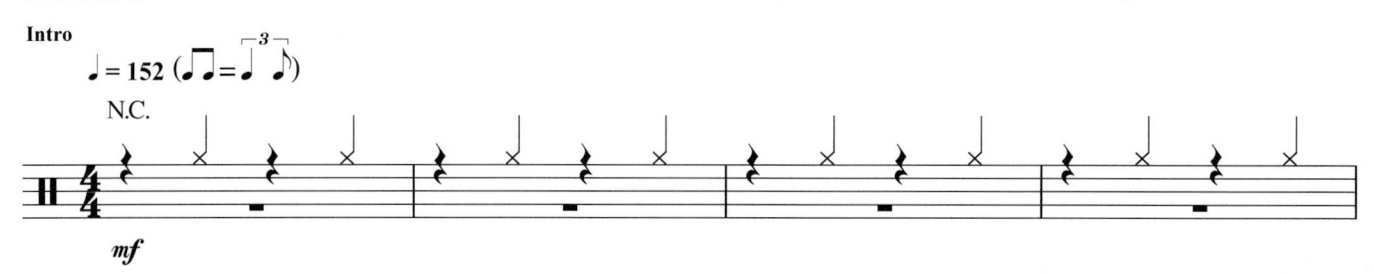

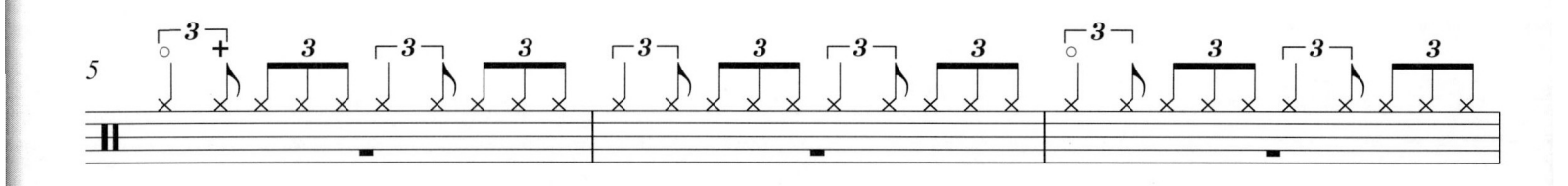

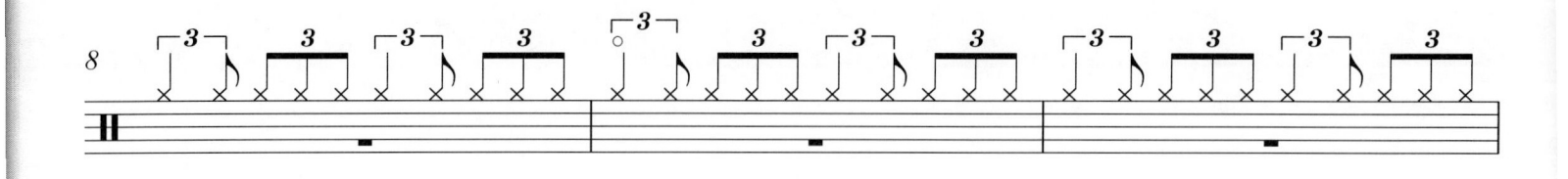

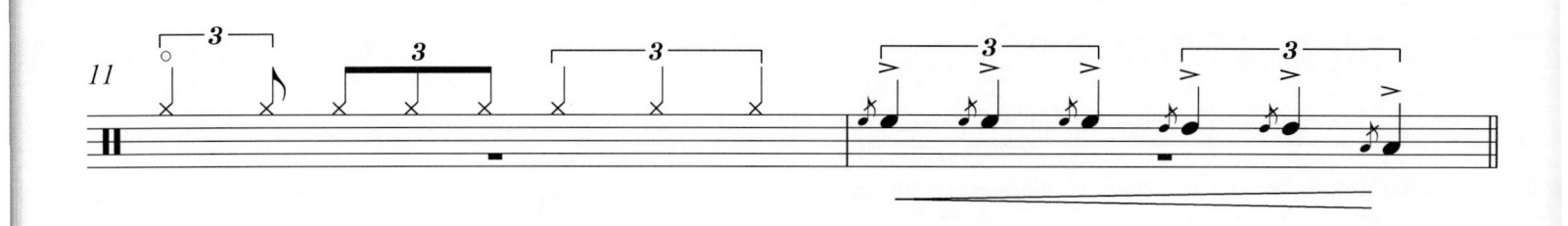

16
D5
C5
20
F5
23
G5
D5
choke
mp
26
C5 D5 C5 D5 C5
D5
C5 D5 C5 D5 C5
29
D5
C5 D5 C5 D5
F5
choke
G5
choke
F5
G5 F5 G5
f
33
D5
C5 D5 C5 D5 C5
D5
C5

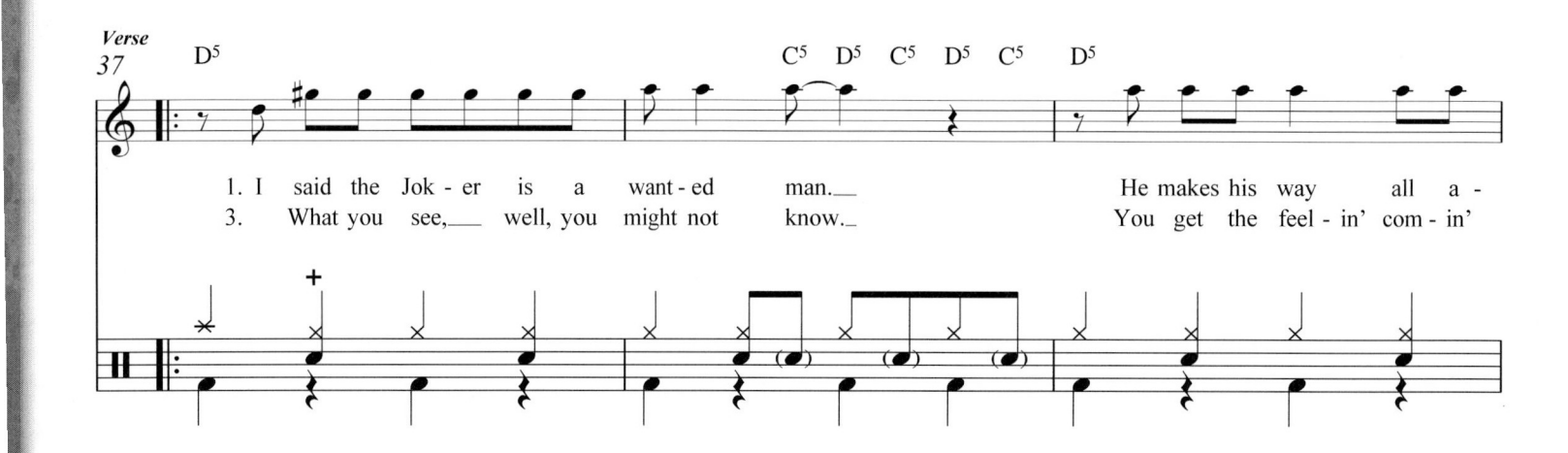

Verse

1. I said the Jok-er is a want-ed man. He makes his way all a-cross the land. I see him sift-ing through the sand, so I'll tell you all the sto-ry 'bout the Jok-er and the Thief in the night.

3. What you see, well, you might not know. You get the feel-in' com-in' af-ter the glow. The vag-a-bond is mov-in' slow, so I'll tell you all the sto-ry 'bout the Jok-er and the Thief in the night.

Verse

2. He's al-ways laugh-ing in the midst of pow - er, al - ways liv-ing in the fi - nal ho - ur.
4. All the peo - ple that you see in the night___ hold their dreams up to the light.___

There is al - ways sweet in the so - ur, so we are not go - ing
The wild - er beast is search-ing for sight___ and we are not go - ing

Chorus

home.
home.

Can you see___ the Jok - er fly - ing o - ver?

64
D5
As she's stand - ing in a field of
67
C5
clo - ver,
F5
watch - ing out
70
G5
ev - 'ry day. I won - der what would hap - pen if he took her a - way.
1.
73
D5
choke
C5 D5 C5 D5 C5 D5
78
D5
C5 D5 C5 D5 C5
2.
took her a - way.

THE PRETENDER
FOO FIGHTERS
GRADE 5 STANDARD

'The Pretender' was the first single from the album *Echoes, Silence, Patience & Grace* released by the American alternative rock band Foo Fighters in 2007. This song was nominated for Best Rock Song, Record of the Year and won Best Hard Rock Performance in the 2008 Grammy Awards. The singer and lead guitarist of the band is Dave Grohl, who prior to the Foo Fighters was the drummer in the legendary grunge band Nirvana.

SONG STATS
Style: Alternative Rock
Tempo: ♩=175

If you like power drumming, this song is for you. Solid technique and coordination will be required as well as stamina when performing this song. The introduction section might look easy on the page, but maintaining a consistent pulse without the anchor hi-hat can be challenging. Try playing the crotchet snare (from bar 1) with the left hand and, if it feels uncomfortable, try it with the right hand. Whichever feels more natural can be used as long as the sound produced is convincing and consistent.

Foo Fighters

In bar 30, the change from hi-hat to the bell of ride should be smooth and followed by a swift movement to the crash cymbal in bar 34. Ensure that the dynamic level remains consistent during these changes in the groove. The only notated dynamic drop in the song is in bar 69 where *mp* is indicated. From that moment, the part gradually builds up in volume and intensity until the end of the piece. Pay attention to the hi-hat notation and remember to let the hi-hat cymbal 'sizzle' when 'loose hats' is indicated. This will help you enhance the stylistic sound produced by the Foo Fighters' drummer.

The geography of the track should be looked at before any specific detail is tackled. All the section repeat signs, first and second time bars and individual bars repeat signs should be noted, as it can be challenging to notice when playing with the backing track at the speed of 175 bpm. If it will make things easier, use a highlighter pen.

The 'Sizzle' sound can be created by playing and maintaining the hi-hat in a loose or half open position. In this position, the hi-hat cymbals are constantly in contact and lead to this stylistic sound.

SUGGESTED LISTENING

Listen to this song by the Foo Fighters as well as some of their earlier hits, 'Monkey Wrench' and 'Everlong', for good examples of Dave Grohl's drumming style.

THE PRETENDER

Words & Music by Dave Grohl, Taylor Hawkins, Nate Mendel & Chris Shiflett
© Copyright 2007 Songs Of Universal Inc./Living Under A Rock Music/I Love The Punk Rock Music/M.J.-Twelve Music/Flying Earform Music.
Universal Music Publishing Limited/Universal/MCA Music Limited/Bug Music Limited.
All Rights Reserved. International Copyright Secured.

19
E G5 A Am
Spin - ning in - fi - ni - ty, but
loose hats
22
D/F♯
the wheel is spin - ning me. It's nev - er end - ing,
2
2
26
Fsus2
E G5 A D5
nev - er end - ing. Same old sto - ry.
Chorus
30
(Am(add 9))
(D9/F♯)
What if I say I'm not like the oth - ers? What if I say I'm not just an - oth - er one
bell of ride
34
(Fmaj7)
of your plays? You're the pre - tend - er. What if I say I will nev - er sur - ren - der?

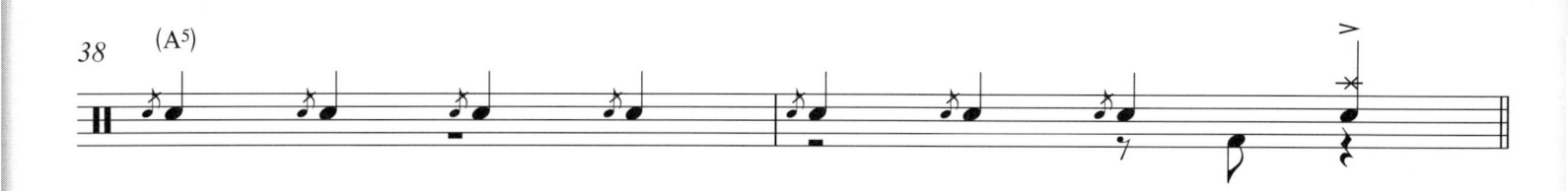

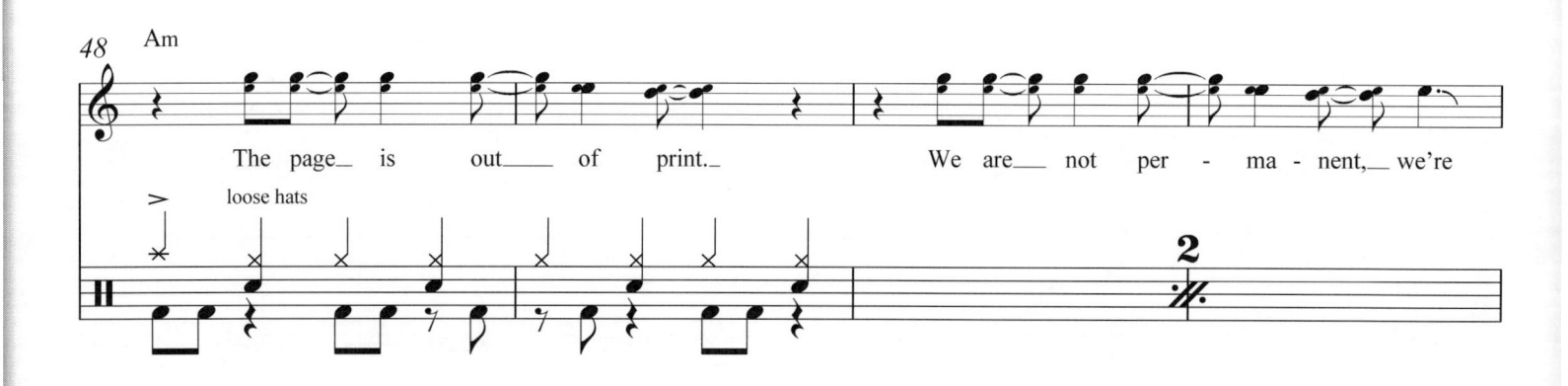

Verse

40 Am

3. In time, or so I'm told, I'm just an-oth-er soul for sale.

loose hats

44 D/F♯   F sus2   E G5 A

Oh, well.

48 Am

The page is out of print. We are not per-ma-nent, we're

loose hats

52 D/F♯   F sus2

tem - po - rar - y, tem - po -

55
E G5 A D5
-rar - y. Same old sto - ry.
Chorus
58
(Am(add 9))
(D9/F#)
What if I say I'm not like the oth-ers? What if I say I'm not just an-oth-er one
bell of ride
62
(Fmaj7)
1.
of your plays? You're the pre-tend-er. What if I say I will nev-er sur-ren-der?
2.
66
F5
D5
nev-er sur-ren-der?
69
A5
I'm
I'm
mp

73
A5
the voice inside your head (that) you refuse to hear.
the face you have to face mirrored in your stare.
I'm
mf
77
A5
what's left. I'm what's right. I'm the enemy. I'm
81
the hand that will take you down, bring you to your knees. So who
loose hats
85
are you? Yeah, who are you? Yeah, who
89
are you? Yeah, who are you?
loose hats
f

MASTER OF PUPPETS
METALLICA
GRADE 5 STANDARD

Metallica

Master of Puppets was the third studio album, released in 1986, by the American heavy metal band Metallica. The first single from this album was released under the same name and became one of Metallica's most popular and identifiable songs. As of June 2012, 'Master of Puppets' has been performed live by Metallica 1,400 times and therefore is the most played song in the history of the band.

This song is a good choice if you want to demonstrate fast tempo metal drumming and control of changing time signatures. As with most Metallica songs, it will be best to divide the track into sections and practise these individually before putting it all together and attempting it with the backing track.

SONG STATS
Style: Metal
Tempo: ♩ = 212

The most challenging section begins in bar 39 and includes changes from $\frac{4}{4}$ to $\frac{5}{8}$. $\frac{5}{8}$ indicates that there are only five quavers in this bar. The main challenge is counting this bar in fast tempo and moving between the time signatures with fluency. To break it down, you will be playing on the first, second and fourth quavers in the bar before returning to the $\frac{4}{4}$ groove. It might be easier to listen to the full backing track a few times before attempting to play it.

Next, have a look at the section that begins in bar 82 which involves changes from $\frac{4}{4}$ to $\frac{2}{4}$. The notated crashes at the beginning of most bars should help you identify where the 'one' is and maintain the synchronisation to the backing track. The frequent 'choke' cymbals in this song require fast hand movement. Focus on achieving the most efficient movement without affecting the timing.

Most of this track should be played loudly. However, there is a crescendo fill in bars 13-15 that allows you to demonstrate your dynamic control. When playing this fill, start moderately quiet (***mp***), then gradually increase the volume until you reach loud (***f***) towards the end of the fill. Starting the fill at the top of the snare drum and moving gradually towards the middle will assist you in creating this dynamic change naturally.

SUGGESTED LISTENING

Listen to the band perform this song live and get a feel for the groove they maintain throughout the time signature changes.

Choke: After hitting the crash cymbal you need to catch it and stop it from ringing (choke).

MASTER OF PUPPETS

Verse

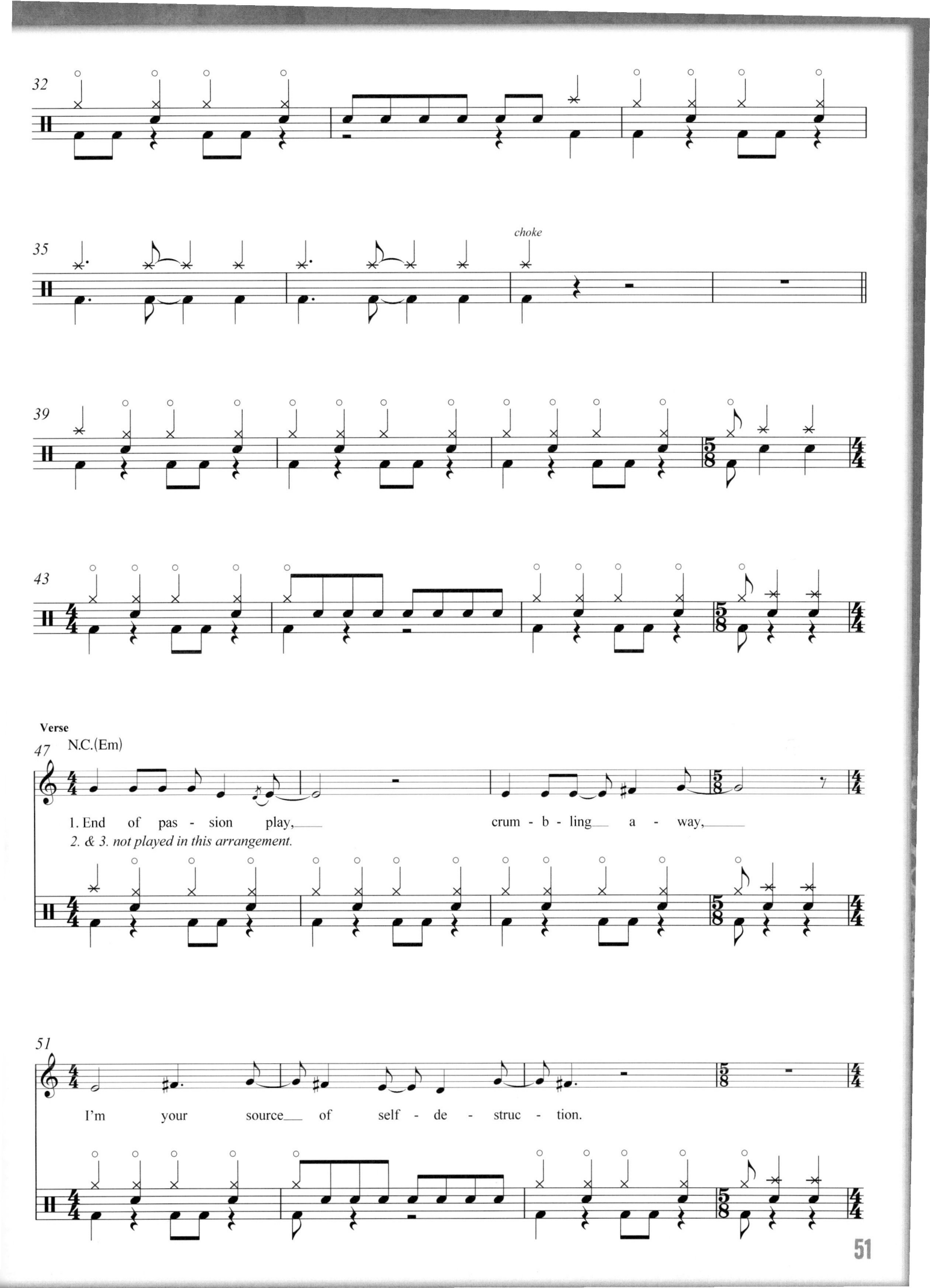

1. End of pas - sion play,___ crum - b - ling___ a - way,___
2. & 3. not played in this arrangement.

I'm your source___ of self - de - struc - tion.

55
Veins that pump_ with fear,___ suck - ing dark - est clear,___
59
lead - ing on___ your death's_ con - struc - tion.
63
N.C.(F#m)
Taste me, you___ will see,___ more is all___ you need,_
66
___ ded - i - cat - ed to___
69
B5
how I'm kill - ing you.___

72
E5 D5 E5 C5 B5 C5 D♯5 B5
Come crawl - ing
(2º) mas - ter, your life burns
76
E5 D5 E5 C5 B5 C5 D♯5 B5
(1º)
(2º)
fast - er, o - bey your
fast - er o - bey your
Chorus
80
E5 F E5
mas - ter, mas - ter. Mas - ter of pup - pets, I'm pull - ing your
choke
choke
84
G C5 B5
strings, twist - ing your mind and smash - ing your
88
A5 D C5
dreams. Blind - ed by me, you can't see a

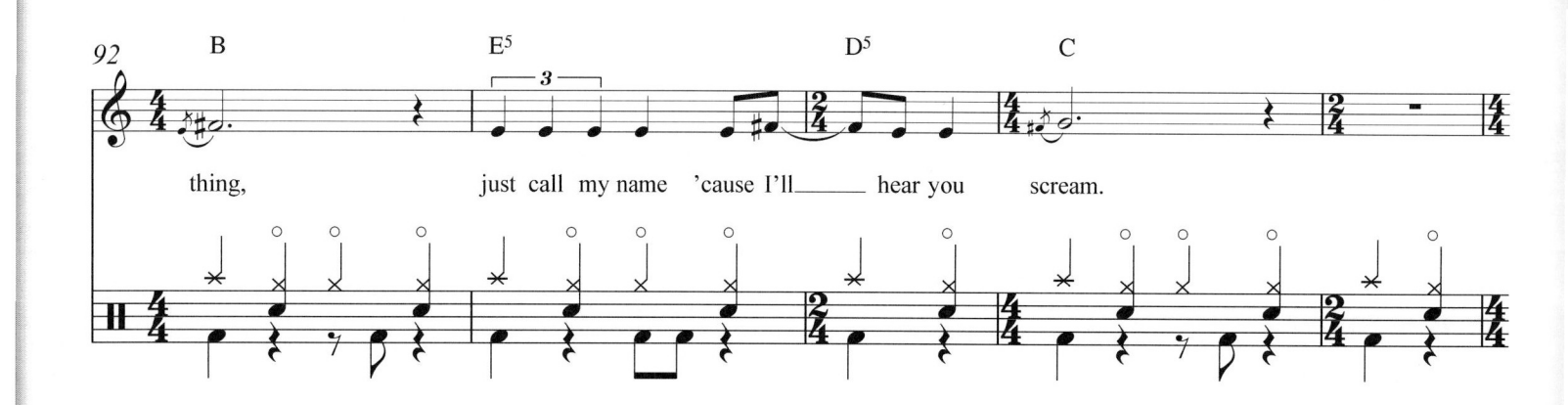

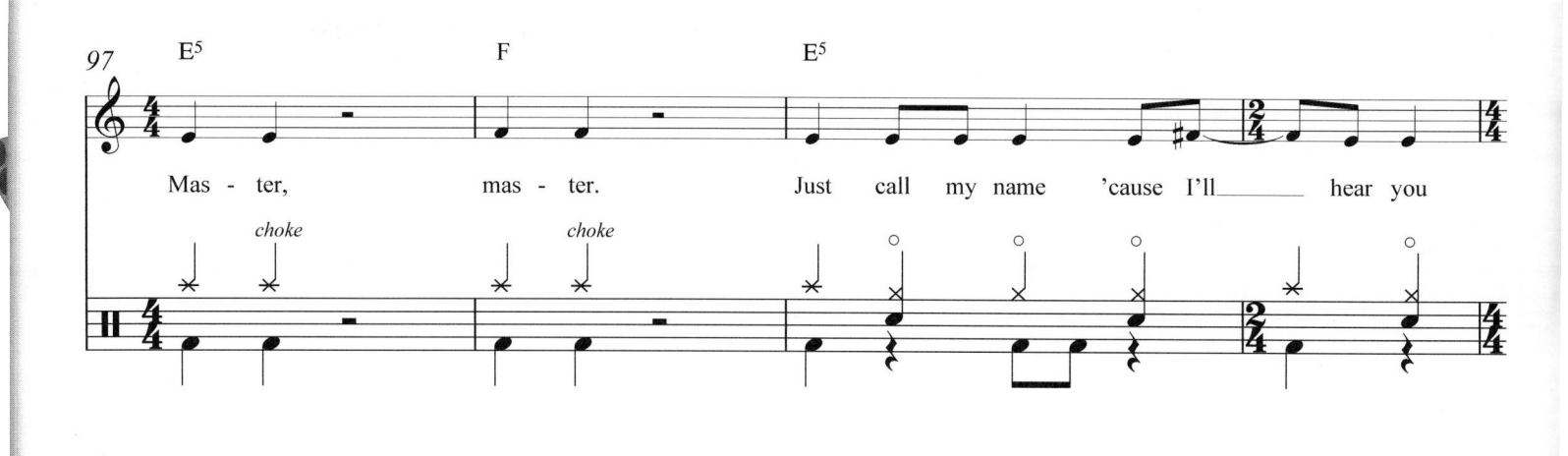

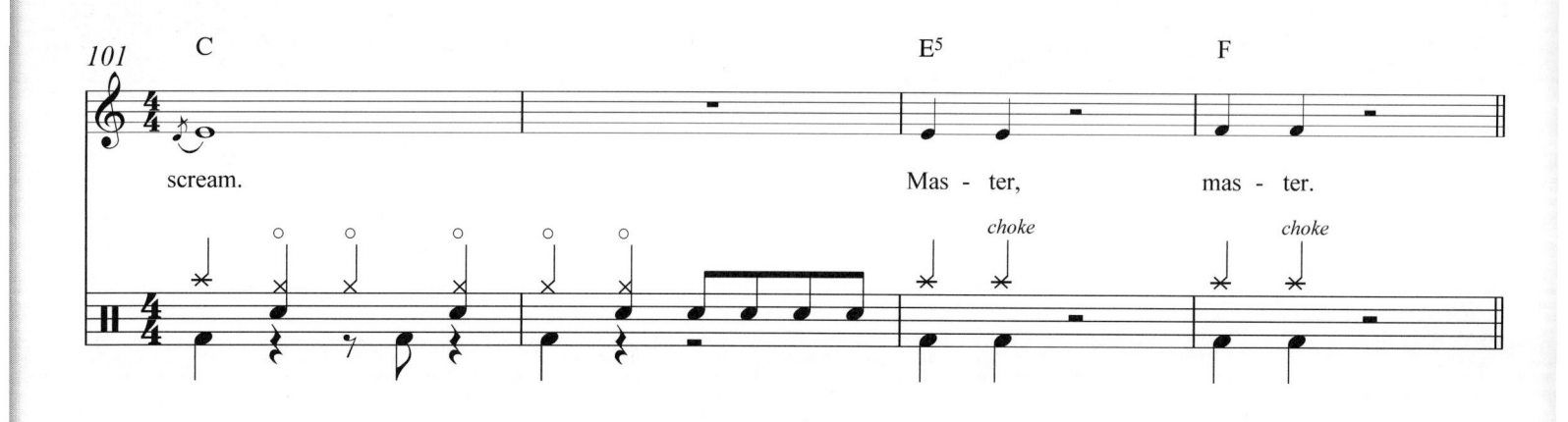

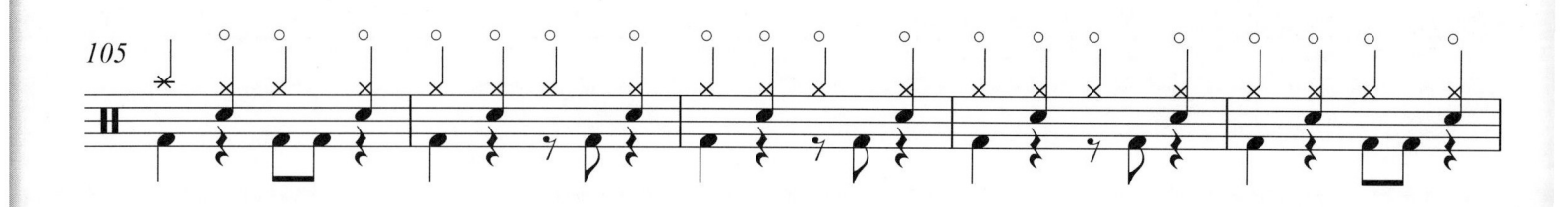

thing, just call my name 'cause I'll hear you scream.

Master, master. Just call my name 'cause I'll hear you

scream. Master, master.

SOMEBODY TOLD ME
THE KILLERS
GRADE 6 STANDARD

The Killers

The American rock band The Killers was formed in 2001 in Las Vegas, Nevada. To date, the band has released four studio albums and sold over 15 millions records worldwide. 'Somebody Told Me' was the debut single from the album *Hot Fuss* and reached Number 1 in the UK Indie Singles chart as well as Number 51 in the US Billboard Hot 100. The song was nominated for Best Rock Song and Best Rock Performance by a Group in the 2005 Grammy Awards.

This is a good song to choose if you want to challenge yourself with inspiring fast tempo rock drumming. As with most of Ronnie Vannucci Jr.'s drumming, there is more than one main groove and frequent changes and developments in each section. Many of the fills and accents correspond musically to the other parts played on the track, so getting familiar with the original recording will be a good way of starting to learn the song.

SONG STATS
Style: Indie Rock
Tempo: ♩=138

SUGGESTED LISTENING
Watch the promotional music video for this song, and note the drummer's technique throughout the fast pace.

This is the hardest piece in the book and is beyond what is required in any GCSE syllabus. Only choose this piece if you are confident that you can deliver it well – a slightly easier piece played well and comfortably will get you more marks than a harder piece played less well.

The toms section from bar 13 can be challenging at first. Start by practising each bar separately and at a slower tempo. Observe the dynamic changes, accents on the ride cymbal and the syncopated push at the end of bar 20. When you feel ready, put it all together and aim to produce a consistent and convincing rock sound from the kit. The added hi-hat pattern from bar 28 will require planning with regards to sticking and advance coordination abilities, so pay special attention to the synchronisation with the backing track at this point.

In the choruses, the offbeat open hi-hat groove is introduced. This will require exact timing and advanced hand-foot coordination. Whether you use the heel up or heel down technique with your hi-hat foot, you should allow time for your body to practise and memorise the movement. Aim for the most efficient and logical movement, as this will be sustainable for longer periods of time. The added semiquavers on the hi-hat from bar 40 can be achieved by moving the left hand from the snare to the hi-hat. Another option will be playing all the hi-hat notes with the right hand, but this will require phenomenal technique and speed.

SOMEBODY TOLD ME

Words & Music by Brandon Flowers, Dave Keuning, Mark Stoermer & Ronnie Vannucci
© Copyright 2004 Universal Music Publishing Limited.
All Rights Reserved. International Copyright Secured.

place like this. An-y-thing goes but don't blink, you might miss.

25 E♭m | G♭ | B♭m
'Cause hea-ven ain't close in a

28
place like this. I said a- hea-ven ain't close in a place like this.

Pre-chorus
31 G♭ | A♭sus | B♭m | B♭sus2 | B♭m
Bring it back down, bring it back down to-night.

35 G♭ | A♭sus
Nev-er thought I'd let a ru-mour ru-in my moon-light. Well, some-bo-dy told

Chorus
39
B♭m
G♭
A♭
— me, you had a boy - friend, who looked like a girl - friend that I had in Feb -
42
F
B♭m
G♭
- ru - a - ry of last — year. It's not con - fi - den - tial, I've got po - ten -
45
A♭
N.C.
Verse
B♭m
- tial. Rea - dy let's roll — on - to some - thing new, —
mf
49
E♭m
tak - ing its toll, — then I'm leav - ing — with - out you. —
f
52
G♭
B♭m
'Cause hea - ven ain't close — in a place like — this. — I said a -

55
-hea-ven ain't close_ in a place like_ this._
Pre chorus
G♭
Bring it back down,
58
A♭sus
bring it back down to-night._
B♭m
B♭sus2
B♭m
G♭
Nev-er thought I'd_ let a
62
ru-mour_ ru-in my_ moon-light._
A♭sus
Well, some-bo-dy told_
Chorus
65
B♭m
_me, you had a boy-friend,
G♭
who looked like a girl-friend
A♭
that I had in Feb-ru-a-ry of last
F
69
B♭m
_year. It's not con-fi-den-tial,
G♭
I've got po-ten-tial.
A♭
A-rush-ing and rush-ing a-round.
F

Bridge

Pace yourself from me, I said maybe baby, please. But I just don't know now, (baby, baby), when all I wanna do is try. Well, somebody told

Chorus
88
B♭m G♭ A♭ F
— me, you had a boy - friend, who looked like a girl - friend that I had in Feb - ru - a - ry of last
92
B♭m G♭ A♭
— year. It's not con - fi - den - tial, I've got po - ten - tial. A - rush - ing and rush -
95
F B♭m G♭
(2° only)
- ing a - round. Well, some - bo - dy told ___ me, you had a boy - friend, who looked like a girl -
98
A♭ F B♭m
- friend that I had in Feb - ru - a - ry of last ___ year. It's not con - fi -
101
G♭ A♭ F B♭m
- den - tial, I've got _ po - ten - tial, a - rush - ing and rush - ing a - round. ______

Series editor: Andrew S. Coxon

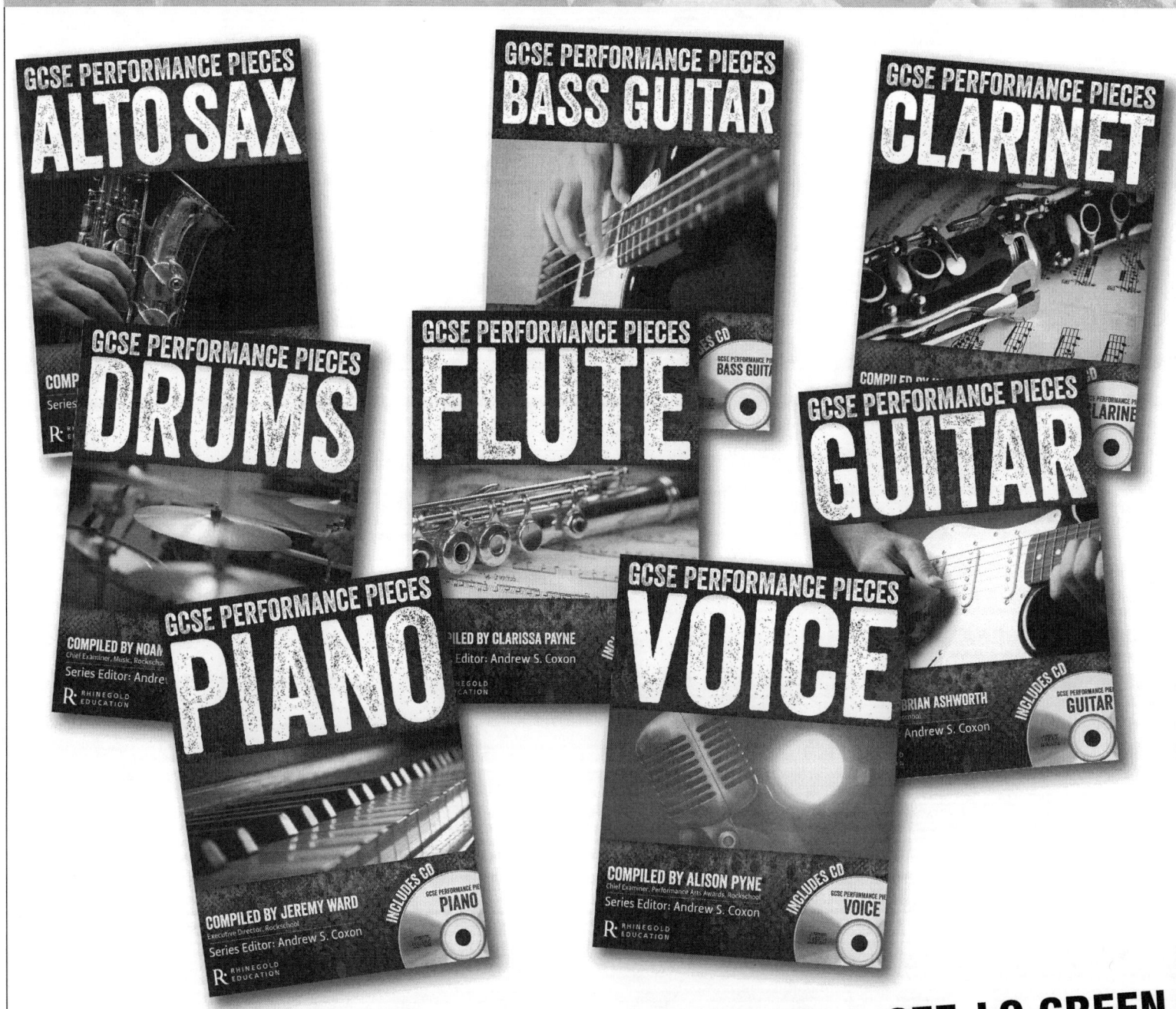

GCSE PERFORMANCE PIECES
- ALTO SAX
- BASS GUITAR
- CLARINET
- DRUMS
- FLUTE
- GUITAR
- PIANO
- VOICE

Featuring: **TAKE THAT • COLDPLAY • CEE-LO GREEN**

R· RHINEGOLD EDUCATION — Order now and get 10%* discount!

To order GCSE Performance Pieces go to www.musicroom.com/rhinegold.
All schools can receive 10% off every order*, plus FREE P&P!**

* Register as an educator online at www.musicroom.com – minimum spend £25
** On all orders over £15

GCSE Performance Pieces

Exciting contemporary repertoire levelled specifically for GCSE performance

Accompanied by expert commentary to help your students prepare, this series will enable GCSE performers to achieve their potential with material they really want to play.

- Covering a range of popular instruments, the series has been compiled by experienced instrumental teachers and for the rock instruments by examiners from Europe's no. 1 rock exam board, Rockschool, and all have been approved by our series editor, a senior GCSE examiner.
- Suitable for all exam boards, each book contains ten songs and covers a range of difficulty appropriate for GCSE level.
- Each book contains access to professional backing tracks, and the songs have been carefully chosen to provide students with the best opportunity to show off their instrument and skills, with a broad range of artists and styles ranging from current chart toppers like Take That, Coldplay, Cee-Lo Green and Adele to the classic greats like the Beatles, Bon Jovi, Oasis and Led Zeppelin.

ADELE • THE BEATLES • BON JOVI • OASIS • AND MORE!

GCSE Performance Pieces: Piano
CODE: RHG533
ISBN: 9781780386355

GCSE Performance Pieces: Voice
CODE: RHG534
ISBN: 9781780386362

GCSE Performance Pieces: Alto Sax
CODE: RHG535
ISBN: 9781780386379

GCSE Performance Pieces: Clarinet
CODE: RHG536
ISBN: 9781780386386

GCSE Performance Pieces: Flute
CODE: RHG537
ISBN: 9781780386393

GCSE Performance Pieces: Guitar
CODE: RHG538
ISBN: 9781780386409

GCSE Performance Pieces: Bass Guitar
CODE: RHG539
ISBN: 9781780386416

GCSE Performance Pieces: Drums
CODE: RHG540
ISBN: 9781780386423

ONLINE TRACK LISTING

1 TAKE ME OUT
(Kapranos/McCarthy)
Universal Music Publishing Limited

2 DON'T LOOK BACK IN ANGER
(Gallagher)
Sony/ATV Music Publishing (UK) Limited

3 LIVIN' ON A PRAYER
(Jovi/Sambora/Child)
Universal Music Publishing Limited/Sony/ATV Music Publishing (UK) Limited

4 NO ONE KNOWS
(Homme/Oliveri/Lanegan)
Universal Music Publishing Limited/EMI Music Publishing Limited

5 SOUL MAN
(Hayes/Porter)
Warner/Chappell Music Limited/Universal Music Publishing Limited

6 COME TOGETHER
(Lennon/McCartney)
Sony/ATV Music Publishing (UK) Limited

7 JOKER & THE THIEF
(Stockdale/Ross/Heskett)
Universal Music Publishing Limited

8 THE PRETENDER
(Grohl/Hawkins/Mendel/Shiflett)
Universal Music Publishing Limited/Universal/MCA Music Limited/Bug Music Limited

9 MASTER OF PUPPETS
(Hetfield/Ulrich/Burton/Hammett)
Universal Music Publishing Limited

10 SOMEBODY TOLD ME
(Flowers/Keuning/Stoermer/Vannucci)
Universal Music Publishing Limited